LIFE CYCLES

Dandelions

by Robin Nelson

Lerner Publications Company · Minneapolis

This is a **dandelion**.

How do dandelions grow?

First, a dandelion **seed** is blown by the wind.

The seed lands on the ground.

Roots grow into the ground, and a **stem** grows up.

The stem grows small leaves.

Then the stem grows long
leaves.

Next, a **flower bud** grows at the top of the stem.

The yellow flowers open.

They close at night.

One day, the flowers stop opening.

Seeds form inside the bud.

Then the bud opens again.

The yellow flowers have
turned into fluffy, white seeds.

The wind will blow the seeds away.

Those seeds will grow new dandelions.

Dandelions

Dandelions can be found all over the world. They first grew in Asia and Europe. People brought them to new countries as food. The dandelions in their gardens spread in the wind. Now dandelions grow everywhere.

Each dandelion plant can live for many years. Every summer, it will grow more dandelion flowers.

Dandelion Facts

 Some people eat dandelion flowers and young dandelion leaves.

 The word *dandelion* comes from a French word that means "lion's tooth." The edges of the dandelion's leaves look like teeth.

 Some people like to blow the white seeds of a dandelion and make a wish. It won't make your wish come true, but it might make more dandelions.

Each petal of a dandelion is a flower. One dandelion bud holds hundreds of flowers.

Many people say that dandelions are weeds because they grow fast and are hard to stop from spreading.

Sometimes animals or a lawn mower will cut off the flowers of a dandelion. But the flowers will always grow back.

Glossary

 bud – a flower that has not opened yet

 dandelion – a plant with yellow flowers and long leaves

 flower – the part of a plant that makes seeds

 seed – what a new plant grows from

 stem – part of a plant that grows above the ground

Index

The images in this book are used with the permission of: © Iakov Kalinin/Dreamstime.com, pp. 2, 22 (second from top); © Ivan Mikhaylov/Dreamstime.com, p. 3; © Dwight Kuhn, pp. 4, 6, 22 (bottom); © Jerome Wexler/Visuals Unlimited, Inc., pp. 5, 22 (second from bottom); Ohio State Weed Lab Archive, The Ohio State University/www.forestryimages.org, p. 7; © Julie Caruso, p. 8; © age fotostock/SuperStock, pp. 9, 15, 22 (top); © Dmitri Melnik/Dreamstime.com, pp. 10, 17, 22 (third from top); © Karlene Schwartz, pp. 11, 14; © Philippe Clement/naturepl.com, p. 12; © Perennou Nuridsany/Photo Researchers, Inc., p. 13; © Kim Taylor/naturepl.com, p. 16; Illustrations by © Laura Westlund/Independent Picture Service.

Front cover: © iStockphoto.com/Ingmar Wesemann.

Lerner Publications Company
A division of Lerner Publishing Group, Inc.
241 First Avenue North
Minneapolis, MN 55401 U.S.A.

Website address: www.lernerbooks.com

Library of Congress Cataloging-in-Publication Data

Nelson, Robin, 1971–
    Dandelions / by Robin Nelson.
        p.   cm. — (First step nonfiction. Plant life cycles)
    Includes index.
    ISBN: 978-0-7613-4069-0 (lib. bdg. : alk. paper)
    1. Common dandelion—Life cycles—Juvenile literature. I. Title. II. Series.
QK495.C74.N445 2009
635'.51—dc22   2008033735

Manufactured in the United States of America
1 2 3 4 5 6 – DP – 14 13 12 11 10 09